98

EVERYDAY MATERIAL
SCIENCE EXPERIMENTS

WATER & OTHER LIQUIDS

Robert C. Mebane
Thomas R. Rybolt

Illustrations by Anni Matsick

TWENTY-FIRST CENTURY BOOKS

A Division of Henry Holt and Company
New York

Twenty-First Century Books
A Division of Henry Holt and Company, Inc.
115 West 18th Street
New York, NY 10011

Henry Holt® and colophon are trademarks of
Henry Holt and Company, Inc.
Publishers since 1866

Library of Congress Cataloging-in-Publication Data

Mebane, Robert C.
Water and Other Liquids / Robert C. Mebane and Thomas R. Rybolt;
illustrations by Anni Matsick.—1st ed.
p.   cm. — (Everyday material science experiments)
Includes bibliographical references and index.
1. Liquids—Juvenile literature. 2. Water—Juvenile literature. 3. Liquids—
Experiments—Juvenile literature. [1. Liquids—Experiments. 2. Water.
3. Experiments.] I. Rybolt, Thomas R. II. Matsick, Anni, ill. III. Title.
IV. Series: Mebane, Robert C. Everyday material science experiments.
QC145.24.M43   1995
530.4'2'078—dc20   94–43154
                                                              CIP
                                                               AC

ISBN 0–8050–2840–4
First Edition 1995

Designed by Kelly Soong

Printed in Mexico
All first editions are printed on acid-free paper ∞.
10 9 8 7 6 5 4 3 2 1

*For Catherine Ramseur with my deepest appreciation
and love*   —R.M.

*For Juanita Harris and Dr. Wayne Harris, in-laws
of choice*   —T.R.

ACKNOWLEDGMENT

We wish to thank Professor Mickey Sarquis of Miami University, Middletown, Ohio, for reading and making helpful comments on the manuscript.

CONTENTS

INTRODUCTION

The world around you is filled with *Air and Other Gases, Water and Other Liquids, Salts and Solids, Metals,* and *Plastics and Polymers.* Some of these materials are part of our natural environment, and some are part of our created, industrial environment. The materials that we depend on for life and the materials that are part of our daily living all have distinct properties. These properties can be best understood through careful examination and experimentation.

Have you ever wondered how a liquid crystal display on a digital watch works, how bleach whitens clothes, why ice floats, or why drops of water are round? In this book you will discover the answers to these and many other fascinating questions about *Water and Other Liquids.* In the process you will learn about water and other liquids as materials—what they are made of, how they behave, and why they are important.

Each experiment is designed to stand alone. That is, it's not necessary to start with the first experiment and proceed to the second, then the third, and so on. Feel free to skip around—that's part of the fun of discovery. As you do the experiments, think about the results and what they mean to you. Also, think about how the results apply to the world around you.

At the beginning of each experiment you will find one or more icons identifying the important physical science concepts dealt with in the experiment. For example, if the icon ✳ appears at the top of the page, it means that matter, one of the basic concepts of science, will be explored. On page 60 you will find a listing of all the icons—matter, energy, light, heat, and electricity—and the experiments to which they relate.

As you carry out the experiments in this book, be sure to follow carefully any special safety instructions that are given. **For some experiments, a ❶ symbol means that you should have an adult work with you**. For all your experiments, you need to make sure that an adult knows what you are doing. Remember to clean up after your experiment is completed.

1

FLOATING ICE

MATTER

MATERIALS NEEDED

Clean plastic container
(such as large
margarine tub)

Refrigerator freezer

Water

Sink

Ruler

Towel

Icebergs are large pieces of ice that have broken off from glaciers or polar ice sheets. Composed mostly of frozen freshwater rather than frozen seawater, icebergs can float many years in the ocean before completely melting. In this experiment you will make a large piece of ice and use it to learn more about icebergs.

Fill a clean plastic container three-quarters full with water. Place the plastic container of water in a freezer and leave it there until all the water has frozen (overnight is long enough).

Remove the container of frozen water from the freezer and place it on the kitchen counter. Fill the sink nearly full with water. Remove the large piece of ice from the container. If the ice does not slip out easily, place the container in the sink of water and leave it there until the large piece of ice is loose.

Place the large piece of ice in the water. Does it sink or float? Use a ruler to measure the height of the ice sticking above the surface of the water, as shown in Figure A. Next, remove the ice from the water and place it on a towel next to the sink with the same

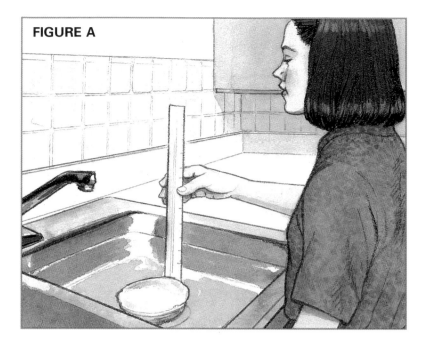

FIGURE A

side on top as when it was floating. Now measure the total thickness of the ice.

To calculate the percentage of ice that is submerged (below the surface of the water), first divide the height of the ice that is above the surface of the water by the total thickness of the ice. Multiply this number by 100 to get the percentage of ice floating above the surface of the water. Subtracting this percentage from 100 gives you the percentage of ice submerged. As an example, if 0.8 in. (2 cm) of ice is floating above the surface of the water and the total thickness of the ice is 7.9 in. (20 cm), then 10 percent (0.8 ÷ 7.9 x 100 percent = 10 percent) of the ice is floating above the surface of the water and 90 percent (100 percent - 10 percent = 90 percent) of the ice is below the surface.

Water is an unusual substance because solid water (ice) has a lower *density* than liquid water. For most substances, the liquid form is less dense than the solid form. Density is the ratio of the amount of a substance (mass) to the amount of space (volume) taken up by the substance. To help clarify, imagine you have 1 cup (0.24 l) each of two different liquids. Let's call them liquid A and liquid B. If liquid A has a greater density (is more dense) than liquid B, then the 1 cup of liquid A will weigh more (have a greater mass) than liquid B. To think of it in another way, say you have separate samples of liquid A and liquid B that have the same weight. If liquid A is more dense than liquid B, then liquid A will have a smaller volume.

A less dense substance will float on a more dense substance. This is why ice floats on water. For nearly every other substance, the solid form will sink in the liquid form. Can you think of a way to test this statement using cooking oil?

In this experiment you should find that 80 percent to 90 percent of your piece of ice is submerged. This percentage will vary depending on the amount of air trapped in the ice. The more air that is trapped, the less dense the ice and the smaller the percentage that is submerged. Ice made from water containing no air is 90 percent submerged in pure water.

The amount of an iceberg that is submerged varies between 80 percent to 86 percent. Usually, Arctic icebergs are more submerged than icebergs originating in Antarctica because Arctic icebergs contain more rocks and gravel, which make the icebergs more dense.

The largest icebergs are found in Antarctica. One particularly large Antarctic iceberg was measured to be nearly 217 mi (350 km) long and 62 mi (100 km) wide. Can you think of any uses for large icebergs?

When icebergs drift into ocean shipping lanes, they become a menace to oceangoing vessels. One of the greatest disasters in ocean travel occurred on April 14, 1912, when the *Titanic*, then the largest ship in the world, struck an iceberg and sank while crossing the Atlantic on its first voyage. More than 1,500 lives were lost in this disaster.

2

POLAR AND NONPOLAR LIQUIDS

ELECTRICITY   MATTER

MATERIALS NEEDED

Balloon

Sink faucet

Wool sweater

Pen

Paper cup

Cooking oil

Have you ever wondered why water and oil do not mix, or how soap combats oily dirt? To learn more about the properties of water and oil, try this experiment. (Note: this experiment works best on a cool, dry day when the humidity is low.)

Begin by inflating a balloon and tying it closed. Turn on a sink faucet and adjust its flow to get a thin stream of water. Rub the balloon on a wool sweater or in your hair to charge the balloon. Move the charged balloon near the stream of water. What happens?

Next, use a pen to punch a small hole in the bottom of a paper cup. Hold the paper cup over the sink and add cooking oil to the cup until a thin stream of oil starts to flow from the hole in the bottom, as shown in figure A. What happens when you bring a charged balloon near the stream of oil?

Both water and oil are made up of *molecules*. Molecules are combinations of atoms held tightly together through chemical bonds. A good analogy for a molecule is a word, which is a combination of letters.

Within molecules are positive and negative charges. If the

positive and negative charges in a molecule are not distributed evenly, one end of the molecule will be slightly negative and the other end slightly positive. Molecules with charged ends are called *polar molecules*. If the positive and negative charges in a molecule are distributed evenly, the molecule is nonpolar.

Rubbing the balloon on a sweater (or in your hair) causes electrons to move from the sweater and collect on the balloon, charging the balloon. Since electrons are negative charges, the balloon becomes negatively charged. You use a charged balloon in this experiment to learn whether water and oil are polar or nonpolar.

When the charged balloon is brought close to the stream of water, the stream bends toward the balloon, showing that water is polar—the positive ends of the water molecules are attracted to the negative charges on the balloon. What would happen if the balloon had a positive charge instead of a negative charge? Since the stream of oil is not affected by the charged balloon, the oil must be nonpolar.

Much of what we call dirt is made up of oil and grease. Water alone will not dissolve oil and grease because water is polar and oil and grease are nonpolar—"like dissolves like." Adding soap or detergent to the water, however, will cause the oil and grease to dissolve.

Soap and detergent molecules are unique in that they each contain a large, nonpolar tail and a smaller, polar head. The nonpolar tail combines with oil and grease and the polar head combines with water. Figure B shows how soap or detergent molecules cause oil to dissolve in water. As you can see in the fig-

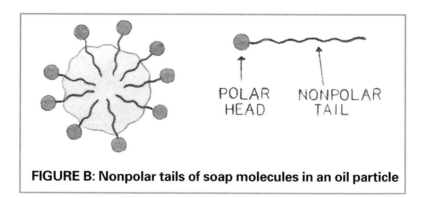

POLAR
HEAD

NONPOLAR
TAIL

FIGURE B: Nonpolar tails of soap molecules in an oil particle

ure, the nonpolar tails of many soap or detergent molecules stick into a tiny oil particle. The polar heads of the soap or detergent molecules stick out into the water, causing the oil particle to be suspended in water. The suspended oil particle can now be washed away with the water.

WATER WETTING

MATERIALS NEEDED

Wax paper

Spoon

Water

Dishwashing liquid

Cooking oil

In this experiment you will explore why water wets (spreads out on) or does not wet a surface.

Place a sheet of wax paper about the size of a piece of notebook paper on a flat surface. Use a spoon to add about 1 teaspoon (5 ml) of water to the wax paper to make a blob of water about the size of a quarter. Slightly lift the edges of the paper and move the blob of water around on the surface of the wax paper. Observe how the water moves across the surface. Touch the wax paper where the water has been. Does the wax paper feel wet?

Now, move the blob of water to the center of the wax paper. Add one drop of dishwashing liquid to the center of the water blob, as shown in Figure A. What happens?

Lift the edges of the wax paper to make the water move across the surface. Touch a spot where the water has been. How does it feel?

You should find that the water blob moves freely across the surface of the wax paper without wetting it. The water molecules in the blob pull together to stay in the shape of a drop. The wax

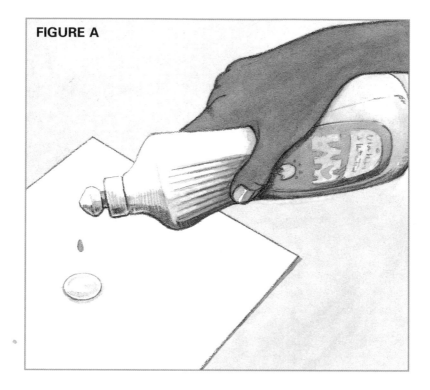

paper does not feel wet even where the large drop of water has passed across the surface.

After the drop of dishwashing soap is added to the water, the behavior of the water should be much different. The soapy water mixture should spread out across the surface rather than staying in a small blob. When you touch the surface over which the water has passed, it probably feels wet. The water did not wet the wax surface. However, the soapy water does.

Water molecules are polar, which means that they each have a positive and a negative side. Molecules of the wax on wax paper are nonpolar, which means that they do not have a positive and negative side. Polar molecules will mix with other polar molecules, just as nonpolar molecules will mix with other nonpolar molecules. However, polar molecules do not mix with nonpolar molecules. The water and wax paper do not mix. The water molecules stay together in the form of a bead or large drop to minimize their contact with the wax paper. They do not spread out on the surface.

Soap molecules are unique because they each have a polar and a nonpolar part. A soap molecule has a long part that is like a wax molecule and is called a tail. It also has a short part that is like a water molecule and is called a head. The head of a soap molecule is polar. The tail of a soap molecule is nonpolar.

When soap is added to water, it causes the water to wet the surface of the wax paper. The heads of the soap molecules attract, or mix with, the water. The tails of the soap molecules are attracted to, or mix with, the wax. Since the soap is attracted to both the water and the wax, it causes the water to spread out across the surface of the wax paper.

Scientists have made a drop of water move uphill against gravity by making one side of a surface underneath the drop polar and the other side nonpolar. The drop of water moves toward the polar side even if it is uphill from the water.

Sometimes we want to make surfaces that cannot be wet with water. For example, car wax is used to make a nonpolar surface on which water will bead up rather than wet the surface. Glass is sometimes coated with a nonpolar substance so water will not stick to the surface and the glass will not "fog up" (become covered with tiny droplets of water).

Sometimes we want to change liquids so that they can be more easily wet by water. Spills of oil into the ocean can damage the environment and harm living things. One of the ways used to clean up oil spills is to add *surfactants* (soaplike molecules) to the oil. A surfactant molecule has a polar and nonpolar part, and thus a surfactant can help the oil mix with the water so it does not wash up on beaches and kill animals.

Try putting a drop of cooking oil on wax paper. Does it wet the surface? Does it stay in a blob or spread out? Based on your observations, do you think oil is polar or nonpolar? Think of other experiments you could do with soap, water, and oil.

4

SKIN MOISTURIZERS

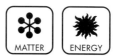
MATTER ENERGY

MATERIALS NEEDED

Two clear plastic cups

Water

Felt pen

Cooking oil

In the United States, billions of dollars are spent each year on lotions and creams to moisturize and relieve dry skin. If you read the labels on several bottles of lotion or cream, you will probably find each contains a number of ingredients, many with long scientific names. Regardless of the ingredients, the way most moisturizing lotions and creams soothe and protect skin is simple, as you will explore in this experiment.

Fill two plastic cups half full with water. Use a felt pen to label one cup *A* and the other cup *B*. Also, mark the water level on the outside of each cup. Slowly pour cooking oil into cup B until the surface of the water is just covered with oil. (See Figure A.) Place both cups in a warm place where they will not be disturbed. Each day for a week, observe how much water is in each cup. What changes do you notice in the water levels during this time? What do you think will happen to the levels after several weeks?

You should find that while the water level decreases in the cup containing only water (cup A), the water level does not significantly change in the cup with the oil layer (cup B). Water easily evaporates from cup A. The thin layer of oil floating on the water in cup B prevents the water in this cup from evaporating.

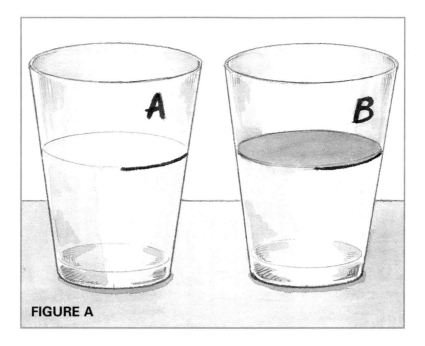

FIGURE A

Water and oil do not mix because their molecules are not attracted to each other. Water molecules are polar and oil molecules are nonpolar. Like molecules attract each other. Unlike molecules have little attraction for each other. Water and oil are unlike molecules. Can you think of other examples of unlike substances?

Water molecules are strongly attracted to each other. This is why water is a liquid under normal conditions. To evaporate, water molecules must have enough energy to escape the attraction of their neighbors. By absorbing heat energy from the room, water in cup A constantly evaporates. Do you think the temperature of the room has an effect on how fast the water evaporates?

Oil molecules require more heat energy than water molecules to evaporate. Usually, cooking oil will evaporate only when it is heated to a high temperature. This is why the cooking oil does not evaporate from cup B.

Some of the water molecules in cup B have enough energy to escape the attraction of their neighbors. When these molecules try to escape, they bump into oil molecules on the surface of the water. They are not able to pass through the layer of oil molecules and do not evaporate.

Moisturizing creams and lotions, which typically contain mineral oil or petroleum jelly, work in much the same way as the layer of oil on the water in this experiment. They help prevent water from evaporating from the skin.

Healthy skin contains about 10 percent moisture. When skin has a lower moisture content, it becomes dry and flaky. Skin protects itself from loss of water by secreting an oil that forms a film on the skin. This natural skin oil can be removed by exposure to sun and wind as well as by washing. Moisturizing creams and lotions replace the natural oil in the skin and prevent or slow the evaporation of water from the skin.

Can you think of other ways of using oil to prevent or slow the evaporation of water?

5

LUBRICATING LIQUID

MATTER HEAT

<table>
<tr><td>

MATERIALS NEEDED

Two aluminum pie pans

Household oil (such as 3-In-One)

</td></tr>
</table>

What is a lubricant and how does it fight friction? To find out, try this experiment.

Hold the two pie pans, one in each hand, so that the bottoms of the pans touch. Rub the pans back and forth for 15 to 30 seconds, as shown in Figure A. What do you feel?

Next, place 5 or 6 drops of household oil on the bottom of one of the pie pans while holding it flat. Again, rub the bottoms of the two pie pans together for 15 to 30 seconds. Now what do you feel?

You should discover that when rubbed together, the bottoms of the two pie pans resist sliding over each other. Depending on how hard you rub the two pans together, you may find that considerable heat is generated in the process. In contrast, when there is a thin layer of oil between the two pan bottoms, you should find that not only do the pans slide over each other much more easily, but there is considerably less heat generated.

The natural resistance encountered when objects move or slide over each other is known as friction. Left uncontrolled, friction causes increased wear of the surfaces in contact with each other and, over time, may destroy the moving objects. As you

FIGURE A

found in this experiment, lubrication with oil can significantly reduce the friction between moving parts. To better understand the origin of friction and how a lubricant like oil can reduce it, let's first consider what a solid surface is really like.

Even with the most modern tools and equipment, it is not possible to make a surface that is truly smooth. Imagine you have a piece of metal that appears smooth. If you could shrink yourself to the size of atoms, the surface of the metal would look like a huge jagged mountain range. When two pieces of metal rub over each other, the jagged areas on the surfaces snag on each other, giving rise to friction.

The most effective way of reducing friction is to keep the rubbing surfaces apart. A simple way to do this is to put a thin layer of oil between the two surfaces. The sliding surfaces are now cushioned by the layer of oil and fewer snags are encountered.

Lubrication of the hundreds of moving parts in a typical

automobile engine requires around 5 qt (4.7 l) of oil. Not only does the oil reduce friction in the engine, it fights metal corrosion, helps remove heat, and provides a seal between the cylinder walls and pistons. Even with lubrication, the moving parts of an engine still develop some friction, which wastes about 20 percent of the power generated by the engine.

The most common liquid lubricants are mineral oils produced during the refinement of crude oil. In jet engines, where very high temperatures develop, special synthetic oils that do not break down at high temperatures are used.

6

VIEWING FALLING WATER DROPS

MATTER · LIGHT

MATERIALS NEEDED

Scissors

Cardboard

Pen

Variable-speed drill

Tape

Paper cup

Water

❗ **Alert! Adult supervision needed. Do not allow the drill or any electric device to get wet.**

Raindrops travel so fast that it is difficult to see their shape. What shape do you think they have? In this experiment you will make a device, called a *stroboscope*, that will allow you to observe falling water drops and to study their shape.

To make your stroboscope, cut a circle about 6 in. (15 cm) in diameter from a piece of cardboard. Punch a small hole in the center of the circle with a pen. Next, cut a rectangular notch out of the circle about 2 in. (5 cm) long and 0.4 in. (1 cm) wide. This notch will serve as a shutter. To finish your stroboscope, push the center hole of the cardboard circle onto the chuck of the drill and secure it to the drill chuck with tape, as shown in Figure A.

Punch a small hole in the bottom of a paper cup with a pen. Fill the cup with just enough water so that water continuously drips from the hole. Can you see the shape of the drops easily, or are they moving too fast?

Next, hold the drill in front of the stream of water drops.

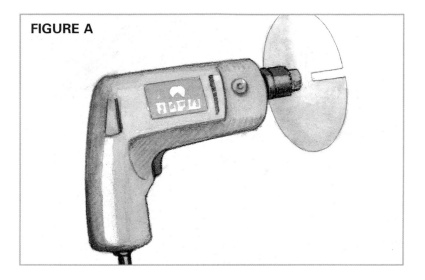

FIGURE A

You may want to ask someone to hold the cup. As shown in Figure B, run the drill on high speed and look through the spinning cardboard circle at the stream of drops. You may find that having bright lights turned on helps you view the drops. What do you see? Does varying the speed of the drill change what you see?

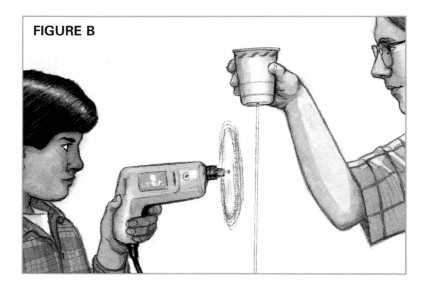

FIGURE B

You should find that the drops of water falling from the paper cup move too fast for you to see their shape. However, when viewed through your stroboscope, the drops of water should appear as nearly perfect spheres moving in slow motion. In fact, you may find that by varying the speed of the drill, you can actually make the spherical drops appear as if they are suspended in air or even moving up to the cup.

With each revolution, the small shutter on your cardboard stroboscope allows your eye only a brief glimpse of the stream of water drops. Because the drill spins the stroboscope much faster than your eyes can react to, the stream of water drops appears to move in slow motion. When the speed of the passing shutter just matches the speed of the falling water drops, the drops will appear to be suspended in air. Can you think of other uses for your stroboscope?

Why is a water drop spherical and not some other shape? To answer this question, you must understand that there is an attraction among the molecules of a liquid and that this attraction keeps the molecules close together. The attraction of a molecule within the liquid is uniform since it is surrounded by neighboring molecules on all sides. The attraction of a molecule on the surface is not uniform because it only has neighboring molecules on one side. As a result of this uneven attraction, there is an inward pull on the surface molecules of a liquid. This inward pull, called *surface tension*, causes the surface to behave somewhat like a skin.

Liquids try to reduce their surface tension by adopting a shape that has the smallest surface area possible. The shape with the smallest surface area is a sphere for any volume. Thus, liquids try to form spherical shapes if they can.

Surface tension not only explains why water drops, including raindrops, are spherical; it explains why some insects can walk on water and why a glass can be filled with water above its rim (try it, but over the sink).

An interesting application of the principle explored in this experiment is the formation of gunshot. Since early times, gunshot has been made by pouring molten metal, usually lead, through a screen atop a tower at least 200 ft (61 m) above a tank of water. As the molten metal drips from the screen, spherical shots form that cool and solidify as they fall to the waiting tank of water. At one time, ball bearings were made the same way.

7

WATER DROPS RIDING ON STEAM

HEAT   MATTER

MATERIALS NEEDED

Stove

Frying pan

Spoon

Water

Oven mitt

❗ **Alert! Adult supervision needed**.

In this experiment you will observe what happens when a drop of water comes in contact with a hot metal surface.

Turn a range-top burner to a high setting. Place a frying pan on top of the burner and wait about 10 minutes to allow the pan to become hot. You may need to lower the setting on the stove if the pan becomes too hot. **Be careful not to touch the hot part of the pan**. Use a spoon to add a drop of water carefully to the hot pan. What sound do you hear? What happens to the drop? **Do not add more than a drop of water at a time to the hot pan**.

Add more drops of water and observe their behavior. Use the oven mitt to hold the handle of the pan. Tilt the pan slightly to make a drop move across the surface of the pan. Can you explain what you see? Turn off the range top and allow the pan to cool.

The boiling point of water, 212°F (100°C), is the temperature at which liquid water is changed to water vapor (steam). Since the temperature of the hot frying pan is probably more than 400°F (204°C), you might expect that a drop of water would instantly change to steam. Instead, the drop lasts a long time in

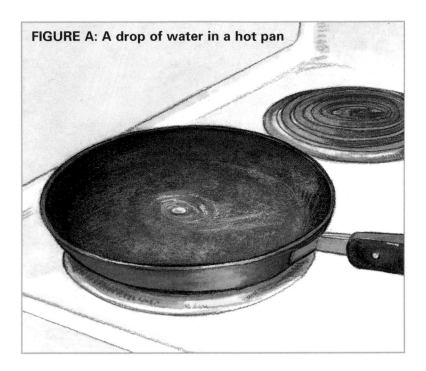

FIGURE A: A drop of water in a hot pan

the hot pan. You probably observe that the drop of water placed on the hot frying pan seems to skate around in the frying pan as it makes a sizzling sound. This surprising behavior of water drops on a hot surface is called the *Leidenfrost effect.*

As the drop of water comes in contact with the metal surface, the outer layer of the drop begins to *vaporize* (change from a liquid to a gas). This water vapor provides a layer of gas upon which the water drop floats. This gas also provides a barrier to the flow of heat from the hot metal pan to the cooler liquid water. As a result, the water drop does not immediately vaporize but instead may take several minutes to change completely to water vapor. The liquid changes to steam, and the drop gradually disappears.

In the Leidenfrost effect, only that part of the drop that touches the hot surface changes to steam. Heat does not flow through gas as well as it does through water. Therefore, the drop is insulated from the hot surface by the steam coming off the drop.

When you tilt the pan, you can make the drop of water move across the surface. As the water drop vaporizes, the gas coming off it gives it a push, just as hot gases coming out of a rocket ship push it through space. As long as gas comes off the drop, it can move around the surface of the pan until all the water has changed to gas.

Allow a drop of water to fall on a metal pan at room temperature. Listen to the sound it makes. Does it make a soft splash? Allow a drop of water to fall on a hot metal pan and listen to the sound. Does it seem to make a hard sound rather than a soft splash? Can you explain why the water sounds different as it hits the hot metal pan? How could the hot steam change the energy of falling and the sound a drop makes?

Have you ever seen pictures or movies of people walking across glowing hot coals? (**Do not try to touch or walk on hot coals.**) How do firewalkers keep their feet from getting burned? Let's discuss several reasons: First, the layer of coals has a high temperature, but the red-hot layer is quite thin. Therefore the total amount of heat energy along the top of a suitable bed of coals is not high. Second, tissue in feet is mostly water, and water can store a lot of heat energy. Therefore, a firewalker's feet can absorb a certain amount of heat without getting burned. Third, the Leidenfrost effect helps insulate the firewalker's feet. Perspiration or moisture on the feet changes to steam and absorbs energy. As you know from your experiment, this steam can act like a layer of insulation. This gas underneath helps protect feet from the effects of the heat. However, even though we understand the science of firewalking, it should only be done by those specially trained in this unique activity.

STORING HEAT FROM MELTING ICE

HEAT **ENERGY**

MATERIALS NEEDED

Paper towel

Bowl

Plastic cup

Water

Watch or clock

Two ice cubes

Have you ever wondered why you can feel comfortable in air that is 70°F (21°C) but feel cool in water that is the same temperature? In this experiment you will compare how air and water differ in their ability to store heat.

Crumple a paper towel into a ball about the size of your fist and place this paper towel in a bowl. Fill a plastic cup about half full with water. Let the cup of water and the bowl with the paper towel sit undisturbed for about 30 minutes. This waiting period is to allow the water to come to the same temperature as the air in the room.

Take two ice cubes of the same size from a freezer. Place one ice cube on the paper towel in the bowl. Place the second ice cube in the glass of water. (See Figure A.)

Watch both ice cubes for about 5 minutes. What happens? Observe the ice cubes again about 5 minutes later. What do you observe?

You will probably observe that the ice cube in the water disappears much faster than the ice cube in the air (on the paper towel). After 10 minutes or less, you may find that the ice in water

FIGURE A

has completely melted while the ice in contact with the air has gotten only a little smaller. Why does the ice in the water melt so much faster than the ice in the air, even though the water and air are at the same temperature? This difference in the speed of melting in water and in air is because water and air have different heat capacities.

Heat capacity is a measure of the ability of a substance to store heat energy. Water has a much higher heat capacity than air. It takes more energy to raise the temperature of water by one degree than to raise the temperature of the same amount of air by the same amount. This difference is because water can absorb, or store, more heat energy than air. Because of the higher heat capacity of water, it is able to transfer, or give, heat energy to the ice cube more quickly, and the ice cube melts faster.

Normal body temperature is 98.6°F (37°C), and if the surroundings are colder than our body temperature we must generate heat to stay warm. If you are in air that is about 70°F (21°C), you will probably feel comfortable because heat is not removed too quickly from your body. However, if you are in water that is 70°F (21°C), it will feel much cooler to you than being in air at the same temperature. The water can remove heat from your body much quicker than the air because of its higher heat capacity.

If you begin to exercise by swimming, you will be comfortable in the water. The water is able to remove heat from your body and keep you from getting too hot. Pools used by swim teams are often kept cool so that swimmers will not get too hot when doing vigorous exercise.

Swimmers need to have heat removed from their bodies, but what happens if your body loses too much heat? *Hypothermia* occurs if a person's body temperature falls below its normal level. If a person is exposed to cold, heat may be removed from the body more quickly than it can be replenished. If this happens, the person's body temperature may fall below normal. As the body temperature falls, the heart rate slows and blood pressure drops. At a lower temperature, the person becomes unconscious. At an even lower temperature, around 60°F (16°C), the heart and brain stop functioning and death results.

Persons with proper clothing outdoors on a cold winter day may be fine unless they slip in water and get wet. Once their clothes are wet they may lose body heat rapidly and can die if they don't get dry and warm. Can you explain why wet clothes make a person more likely to get hypothermia?

ABSORBING MICROWAVE ENERGY

MATERIALS NEEDED

Two microwave-safe
containers

Measuring cup

Sugar

Water

Microwave oven

Oven mitt

Cooking thermometer

❗ **Alert! Adult supervision needed.**

Have you ever wondered how a microwave oven cooks food? In this experiment you will compare the microwave energy absorbed by sugar and water and learn more about cooking with microwave ovens.

Place 1 cup (0.24 l) of sugar in a microwave-safe container. Place 1 cup (0.24 l) of water in a second microwave-safe container. **Never put metal objects into a microwave oven because they could damage the microwave oven when it is operating**. As shown in Figure A, put both containers into a microwave oven and heat on full power for two minutes. Use an oven mitt to remove both containers and place them on a countertop.

Place a cooking thermometer into the container with the sugar. Leave the thermometer in the sugar for about 20 seconds and then check the temperature. What is the temperature of the sugar? Place the cooking thermometer in the second container and measure the temperature of the water. What is the temperature of the water?

You should find after heating in a microwave oven that the water is warm while the sugar remains cool. The temperature of the water may be 150°F (66°C) or higher. However, the thermometer in the sugar will probably not show any change, so the sugar has remained close to room temperature.

Microwaves are a type of electromagnetic energy. Microwave ovens use this energy to cook foods. The microwaves are absorbed by water molecules in food and cause the water molecules to rotate more rapidly. The extra energy of these more rapidly rotating water molecules spreads out and causes other molecules to move more rapidly. This causes the food to get warm and cook. Since the dry sugar does not contain water molecules, it does not absorb the microwave energy.

Microwaves go through glass and paper without heating them. Metal objects reflect microwaves and will damage microwave ovens if placed in them. The walls of microwave ovens are metal to help reflect the microwaves back to the food to be cooked.

A special electronic tube called a magnetron is used to convert the energy of electricity to microwave energy. The microwaves are scattered into the microwave oven by a stirrer that has moving metal blades like a fan. The advantage of microwave cooking is that it is quicker and more energy efficient than conventional electric cooking. In conventional electric cooking an electric current passes through a coil of wire that gets hot because of the resistance of the wire to the current flow.

The amount of heat generated in a microwave oven depends on the amount of water present in the food. In general, the more water, the faster the food cooks. Other liquids such as oil may absorb microwaves, but not as efficiently as water does.

Electromagnetic waves may pass through matter or be absorbed by it. X rays, used to take skeleton pictures, pass through water but are absorbed by bones and lead. Microwaves pass through air and paper but are absorbed by water and reflected by metal. Light passes through air and water but is blocked by paper and metal. Can you list other types of electromagnetic waves?

LIQUID TO SOLID

MATTER HEAT ENERGY

MATERIALS NEEDED

Metal saucepan, medium size

Water

Stove

Paraffin wax (used for canning and candle making; available in most stores)

Metal saucepan, small size

Oven mitt

Hot pad

Meat thermometer (used in cooking)

Plate

Two pieces of note-book paper

Pen

Watch or clock

❶ Alert! Adult supervision needed.

In this experiment you will measure how temperature changes as a liquid is converted into a solid.

Fill a medium-size saucepan about two-thirds full of water. Place this saucepan on the burner of a stove, and turn this burner to a medium-high setting.

Place a block of paraffin wax in the small saucepan. Paraffin wax usually comes in small, flat blocks. One block of paraffin is about the same as a cup of paraffin. Set the small saucepan inside the medium saucepan. The small saucepan will rest on top of the water in the medium saucepan, as shown in Figure A. You heat the paraffin this way so it will not get too hot. Paraffin wax can burn. Do not heat paraffin

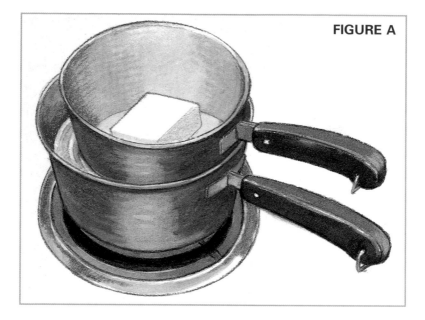

directly on the stove. Always heat it in a pan placed in a second pan of hot water.

Continue heating on the stove until the wax has completely changed from a solid to a liquid. This should take about 10 minutes. Turn off the stove. Use an oven mitt to remove the small saucepan and place it on a hot pad on a countertop. Insert a meat thermometer into the liquid wax. Use the clip attached to the thermometer to clip the thermometer to the side of the pan. Place the saucepan with wax on a plate so that the pan is at a slight angle and the liquid wax is on the side of the pan near the thermometer.

At the top of a piece of notebook paper write "Time (minutes)," and next to it write "Temperature (°F)." Write "0" under "Time (minutes)." Read the temperature off the thermometer and write this value under "Temperature (°F)." Continue to record the time and temperature every 2 minutes for a total of 60 minutes. It may be necessary to continue these readings on a second page. When you record the temperature, record any observations about the wax, such as whether it is still a liquid, is beginning to turn solid, or has turned to a solid.

To remove the thermometer, you may need to heat the wax in the pan again as you did before. You can remove the thermometer when the wax is changed to a liquid.

At what temperature does the wax begin to change to a solid? At what temperature does the wax seem to be completely solid?

The freezing point of water, 32°F (0°C), is the temperature at which liquid water is changed to ice (solid water). You should observe that paraffin wax changes from a liquid to a solid at a much higher temperature than water.

You should observe that the temperature on the thermometer gradually decreases. You may observe that the temperature drops more rapidly while the wax is still a liquid. As the liquid begins to change to a solid, the speed of cooling slows down. This change in cooling occurs because more energy must be removed to change a liquid to a solid than simply to cool a liquid.

Paraffin wax is a mixture of hydrocarbons (molecules that contain carbon and hydrogen atoms). The hydrocarbon molecules are much bigger than water molecules and have strong attractions for other hydrocarbons. These attractions make the molecules in wax stick together to make a solid.

When you heat the paraffin wax, enough heat energy is supplied to change it from a solid to a liquid. When it becomes a liquid, the molecules are free to move past one another and are not locked into fixed positions. As the wax cools, the motion of the molecules slows down. The molecules move more slowly, and when they lose enough energy they go back to solid form. In other words, to change a liquid to a solid you must remove heat energy, and to change a solid to a liquid you must add heat energy.

Paraffin wax is a white to colorless solid that feels greasy. It has a range of melting points rather than one distinct value because it is a mixture of different molecules and not just one type of molecule. The larger the molecules that are used in the mixture, the higher the resulting melting point. Paraffin is used to make wax paper, to make candles, to cover food products in canning, and to waterproof wood.

A heated hair roller provides an interesting application of the use of hot wax to store heat energy. The heated hair roller is made of an outer layer of plastic and a hollow inner core lined with aluminum. In between there is a chamber filled with wax such as beeswax. When the roller is placed on a metal heating element, the roller gets warm and the wax melts. For curling, hair is wound around the hot roller and the roller releases its heat slowly over about 12 minutes.

When the roller is hot, you can shake it and hear a sloshing sound from the liquid wax inside it. If you shake the roller when it is at room temperature, you will hear no sound because the wax is a solid. Wax is used in the roller because it takes more energy to change the wax from a solid to a liquid than just to heat a solid or a liquid to a higher temperature. A roller filled with wax can store more heat energy than a roller without wax. This extra energy is released when the roller cools.

The energy change associated with going from a liquid to a solid has been used to make a small warming device. Thermogel is a supersaturated (extra solid in water) solution of sodium acetate trihydrate. This solution can be used to store energy. This Thermogel solution will remain a liquid until it is initiated, and then it will change to a solid. As this special solution crystallizes to a solid, it gives off heat.

Thermogel can be used over and over. When you add heat by placing a pouch of Thermogel in hot water, the solid Thermogel is changed to a liquid. The liquid cools to room temperature but does not change to a solid until it is initiated. The Thermogel stores the extra energy that can be given off when a liquid changes to a solid. Can you think of other uses of the heat energy associated with changes from solid to liquid or liquid to solid?

11

BENDING LIGHT

LIGHT

MATERIALS NEEDED

Plastic pitcher

Sink

Water

Nickel

Water glass

Pencil

Do you think you can bend light? In this experiment you will try to use water to make light go around a corner.

Place an empty plastic pitcher in a sink under a water faucet so that you can add water to the pitcher without moving it. Put a nickel in the bottom of the pitcher. Move the nickel until it is touching the side of the pitcher toward the front of the sink, as shown in Figure A. Begin with your head directly over the pitcher so you can see the nickel inside the pitcher. Now, slowly move your head back, away from the sink, until the nickel completely disappears. You must stay very still and keep your head in exactly the same place for the rest of this experiment.

While holding your head steady, turn on the faucet to allow water to flow. As the water fills the pitcher, continue to look at the bottom of the pitcher. When the water has nearly filled the pitcher, turn off the faucet to stop the water. Do not move your head. Where is the nickel? Can you see it?

You probably observed that as water was added to the pitcher, the nickel seemed to move. The nickel could not be seen

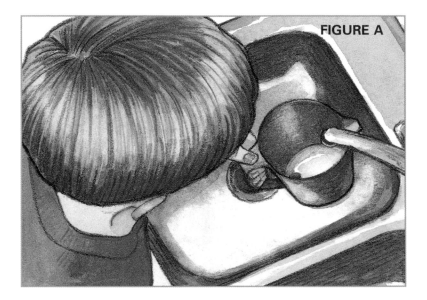

FIGURE A

at all when the pitcher was empty and the side of the pitcher blocked your view. However, when the pitcher was filled with water, you should have been able to see the nickel even though you had not moved your head. Can you explain this change?

In order for you to see the nickel in the bottom of the pitcher, light striking the nickel must reach your eyes. Light normally travels in a straight path, and when the pitcher is empty the light reflected off the nickel travels straight to your eye. When you move your head back, the side of the pitcher blocks the light and you cannot see the nickel. However, when water is added to the pitcher, the light no longer travels in a straight line, but is bent.

Light waves are bent when they travel from water into air or air into water. *Refraction*, the bending of light, occurs whenever light goes from one substance into another. The light is bent when it goes from air to water because light waves travel more slowly in water than in air. Two substances in which light travels at different speeds will cause refraction if the light goes from one substance to the other at an angle (not straight).

Put a pencil in a clear glass that is partially filled with water.

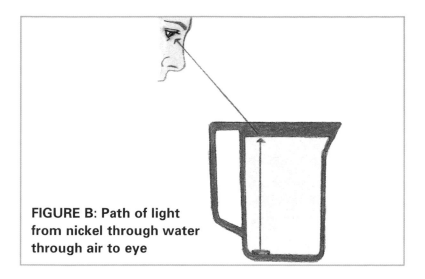

FIGURE B: Path of light from nickel through water through air to eye

Look at the pencil from the side. Does the pencil appear to be broken at the surface of the water? Can you explain why the pencil looks broken?

Scientists use the index of refraction as a measure of how much light bends when it passes from one substance into another. The *index of refraction* is the ratio of the speed of light in a vacuum to the speed of light in a specific substance. This extent of bending can be measured by a device called a *refractometer.* Measuring the index of refraction with a refractometer is one way scientists identify unknown liquids or determine the amount of liquids in a mixture.

When light passes from air into glass and then out of the glass, it can be bent. Different colors of light are not bent by the

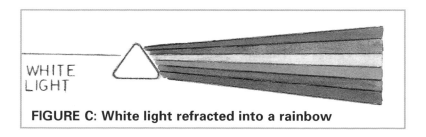

WHITE
LIGHT

FIGURE C: White light refracted into a rainbow

same amount, and so the effect of this bending, or refraction, is to spread white light into the colors of the rainbow: red, orange, yellow, green, blue, indigo, and violet.

A prism is a triangle of glass that uses refraction to split white light into a rainbow of colors. In 1666 Isaac Newton discovered that light could be separated into a rainbow of colors with a prism. He called this rainbow of colors a *spectrum*. Natural rainbows in the sky are also caused by refraction. Droplets of water in the atmosphere act like tiny prisms and spread white light into a spectrum of colors. We usually see rainbows when the sun comes out from behind clouds during or right after a rain.

Do lenses bend light? Can you explain why refraction would be important in making eyeglass lenses or contact lenses? If the natural lens in a person's eye is not the right shape, then the image the person is looking at will not be focused properly at the back of the eye. How do eyeglass lenses or contacts enable people to see more clearly?

12

BLUE
WATER

LIGHT

MATERIALS NEEDED

White bathtub

Clear drinking glass

Water

Earth is referred to as the "blue planet" because of its bluish appearance when viewed from outer space. Perhaps you have seen photographs of Earth taken from outer space during space shuttle missions. The reason the earth appears blue is that much of its surface is covered with water, and water has a blue color. To learn why large bodies of water can have a blue color, try this experiment.

Do this experiment with a white bathtub in a bathroom that does not contain blue colors (for example, in walls and curtains). Fill a clear drinking glass with water. Does the water have color? Next, fill a bathtub a little more than half full with water. What color is the water? Will water temperature have an effect on the color of the water?

Water is naturally blue in color because of its interaction with light. Light from incandescent and fluorescent lamps appears white because it contains nearly all the colors in a rainbow. When white light passes through water, some of the red light in it is absorbed by the water molecules.

The color of a substance is the complement of the color it absorbs. For example, a substance that appears violet absorbs yellow light, and a substance that appears yellow absorbs violet light.

Water appears blue because it absorbs red, the complement of blue. Interestingly, water molecules, which constantly vibrate like springs, vibrate faster when they absorb red light.

Light must pass through a large amount of water before enough red light is absorbed to make the water appear blue. This is why a glass of water appears colorless. Light actually passes through your bathtub of water more than once. It first passes through the depth of water in the tub and is reflected off the bottom (and sides) of the white tub. Some of the light reflected from the bottom of the tub passes back through the water and to your eyes. Thus, if your bathtub is filled to a depth of 6 in. (15 cm), the light you see reflected from the bottom of the tub travels a total of 12 in. (30 cm) in water.

The natural blue color of water is easy to see in deep, clear mountain lakes and clear seas. Holes in deep snow, thick pieces of ice, and glaciers appear blue because of the natural color of water. Bodies of water, such as rivers, that contain large quantities of suspended particles such as silt, tend to be more green than blue. Light scattered by the suspended particles is shifted slightly from blue to green.

COLOR
IN A
SOAP BUBBLE

13

MATERIALS NEEDED

Soap bubble solution

Wand for blowing
bubbles

This experiment works best with bright, natural light, so try to do it outside on a sunny day or in a room that gets plenty of sunlight. Blow a large soap bubble and catch it with the wand. (See figure A.) Closely examine the bubble until it breaks. Repeat several times, describing the changes that take place in each of your bubbles.

The surface of your soap bubbles should appear brilliantly colored. You may also observe that the colors change and move around the bubble. Just before a bubble breaks, you may even notice the formation of black spots on it.

A soap bubble consists of a thin film of soap solution. The average thickness of the soap film in a new bubble is about 0.002 in. (0.005 cm). The thickness of the film decreases with time as water evaporates from the bubble.

When natural light, which contains all the colors of the rainbow, strikes a soap bubble, some of the colors in the white light are reflected by the bubble and other colors pass through the bubble. The thickness of the soap film determines which colors are reflected. A soap bubble with a thickness of 0.002 in. (0.005 cm) reflects all colors except red and blue light. With blue and red missing, a soap bubble appears greenish. For comparison, total

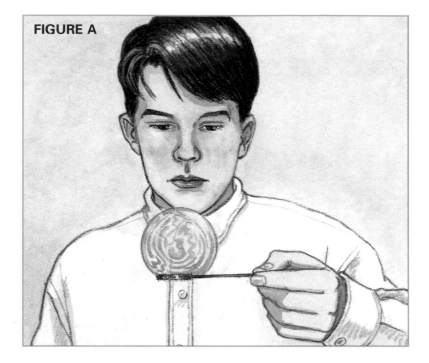

reflection of light by an object makes the object appear white while an object that reflects no light appears black.

The colors reflected by the soap bubble change as the thickness of the soap film decreases with evaporation. Typically, a bubble changes from green to blue as the film becomes thinner. At a thickness of about 0.0012 in. (0.003 cm), no visible light is reflected by a soap film. Areas on a soap bubble that reach this thickness appear black and are usually seen just before the bubble breaks.

The colors seen in thin films of oil floating on water or smeared on dry pavement are caused in a similar manner to the colors of a soap bubble. Minute scales on many beetle wings and butterflies behave like thin films, imparting iridescent colors to these fine structures. The brilliant colors in peacock and pheasant feathers are caused in a similar way. Can you think of other examples around you?

14

LIQUID CRYSTALS

MATTER   HEAT   LIGHT   ELECTRICITY

MATERIALS NEEDED

Package of Duracell batteries with battery tester

Scissors

Coffee cup

Hot water from sink faucet

Thermometer (optional)

Have you ever used the battery tester on a package of Duracell batteries? Do you know how this simple battery tester works? In this experiment you will learn how it works, and you will also learn about an important class of materials called *liquid crystals.*

Use the scissors to cut out the battery tester from a package of Duracell batteries. Fill a coffee cup three-fifths full with hot water from a sink faucet. Dip about 1 in. (2.5 cm) of one end of the battery tester into the hot water. What happens on the front face of the battery tester? What happens to the battery tester when it is removed from the water? Describe how long it takes for any changes to occur when you remove the battery tester from the hot water. Does it matter which end of the battery tester is placed in the hot water? What is the lowest water temperature that will cause the battery tester to change?

The Duracell battery tester consists of a simple liquid crystal display joined to an electrically conducting material. The liquid crystal display is the front of the tester and the electrically conducting material is the back. The tester is normally dark. However, when the tester is dipped in hot water, the portion of the tester under the hot water appears yellow. The yellow color is replaced by the dark color when the tester is removed from the water.

As this activity demonstrates, the liquid crystal display on the battery tester is sensitive to heat. When a battery is tested, electricity flowing through the electrically conducting material from the battery produces heat, which is felt by the liquid crystal display. A good battery will generate enough heat to make most of the liquid crystal display yellow. The battery tester is designed so that the status of a battery is easily determined by the amount of the liquid crystal display that appears yellow. A dead battery produces no heat, so the liquid crystal display remains dark.

Within the liquid crystal display are layers of molecules shaped like rods. These rodlike molecules can align themselves all in one direction, much like matches in a matchbox. A collection of these rodlike molecules is called a liquid crystal.

The molecules in a typical liquid, such as water, are random. The molecules in a typical solid, such as table sugar, are ordered and occupy specific positions in the solid crystal. Liquid crystals are unique substances because although their molecules are ordered like those in a crystal, the molecules can still flow like those in a liquid.

The liquid crystal display on your tester appears dark and murky because the layers of rodlike molecules in the display scatter the light striking it. When the rodlike molecules are heated, they move and change their arrangement. When just enough heat has been added to the molecules, they change their arrangement and light passes through the layers of molecules without being scattered. This exposes a yellow colored strip that is under the liquid crystal display. When the heat is removed and the liquid crystal display cools, the rodlike molecules realign to their original position and the layers of molecules scatter the light again.

There are other liquid crystals that change with electricity instead of heat. Such liquid crystals are common in displays on calculators, digital watches, digital automobile dashboards, and laptop computer screens. A display like that found on a digital watch is shown in Figure A.

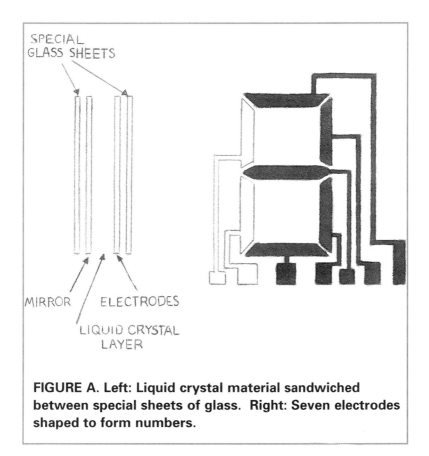

SPECIAL
GLASS SHEETS

MIRROR ELECTRODES

LIQUID CRYSTAL
LAYER

FIGURE A. Left: Liquid crystal material sandwiched between special sheets of glass. Right: Seven electrodes shaped to form numbers.

The liquid crystal material is sandwiched between special glass plates. Overlaying the liquid crystals are seven electrodes arranged so that any digit between zero and nine can be generated. When an electrode is not receiving an electrical signal, the liquid crystal molecules in the display allow light to pass through them and be reflected by a mirror on the bottom of the display. This area under the electrode appears bright. When an electrical signal is sent to an electrode, the liquid crystal molecules change alignment so that light does not pass through them and the area appears dark.

Can you think of other uses for liquid crystals?

DISAPPEARING COLOR

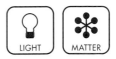

LIGHT   MATTER

MATERIALS NEEDED

Water

Three jars

Measuring cup

Blue food coloring

Spoon

Safety goggles

Liquid laundry bleach, such as Clorox **(use bleach with care— read caution on label)**

⊘ Alert! Adult supervision needed.

In this experiment you will explore the effect of bleach on blue dye in water. Add 1 cup (0.24 l) of water and 5 drops of food coloring to the first jar and to the second jar. Use a spoon to stir the water and food coloring in each jar until they are well mixed.

Caution—bleach can be harmful if not used properly. Do not allow bleach to get on skin or in eyes. Return the bleach container to a safe location (away from young children) when you are finished. Use safety goggles for eye protection when pouring the bleach.

Pour a small amount of bleach into the empty third jar. Using this jar to pour the bleach into the bleach container's cap, add 2 capfuls of bleach to the first jar, as shown in Figure A. Stir the bleach and water mixture. Let the first and second jars sit for 20 minutes while you watch the jars. What do you observe happening?

FIGURE A

After the experiment is complete, pour the liquid from the jars down the sink drain and thoroughly rinse the three jars and the spoon with water.

You should observe that the blue color fades and may disappear completely from the jar with the bleach. The jar with no bleach should not change.

Blue food coloring is made of dye molecules that absorb the red part of white light. This allows only blue light to pass through the liquid, and the color we see is blue.

Bleach reacts with food coloring to change its dye molecules so that they no longer absorb light. Laundry bleach is a chemical that is a strong oxidizer. Blue dye molecules and bleach react in a chemical reaction called *oxidation*. This oxidation reaction changes the dye molecules so that the blue color gradually disappears and the molecules have no color. They no longer absorb light. The blue color gradually disappears because the blue dye molecules are changed.

Many different types of chemicals are used to oxidize or change other molecules. Chlorine gas is an oxidizer used as a disinfectant in water treatment plants to kill bacteria and help make water safe to drink. Hydrogen peroxide can be used to oxidize pigments that give color to hair. Hydrogen peroxide can lighten the color of hair. Chlorine dioxide is used to bleach paper pulp and oxidize pigments in the pulp without damaging the wood fibers. In the textile industry, this bleaching is used to make white paper.

Can you explain why laundry bleach is used in cleaning clothes?

SEPARATING COLORS

MATERIALS NEEDED

Coffee filter (type used in coffeemakers)

Bowl

Green food coloring

Spoon

Water

Can you separate colors that are mixed together in a liquid? In this experiment you will try to separate the colors that are used in the making of green food coloring.

Place a coffee filter upside down in a bowl. The bottom of the coffee filter should stick up in the air, away from the bowl. Add 1 drop of green food coloring to the center of the filter, as shown in Figure A. Use a spoon to add 2 drops of water to the spot of green on the filter. Wait about a minute and add 2 more drops of water to the same spot in the center of the filter. Wait about a minute and observe the filter. What do you see?

You should observe that the water and green color have moved out into the coffee filter. As the water spreads through the filter, it carries the green color with it. However, you should also observe the appearance of other colors—yellow and blue. From the center of the filter outward, you should see rings of yellow, green, and blue, as shown in Figure B.

Green food coloring is made of a mixture of yellow and blue dyes. The yellow dye molecules are attracted more strongly to the

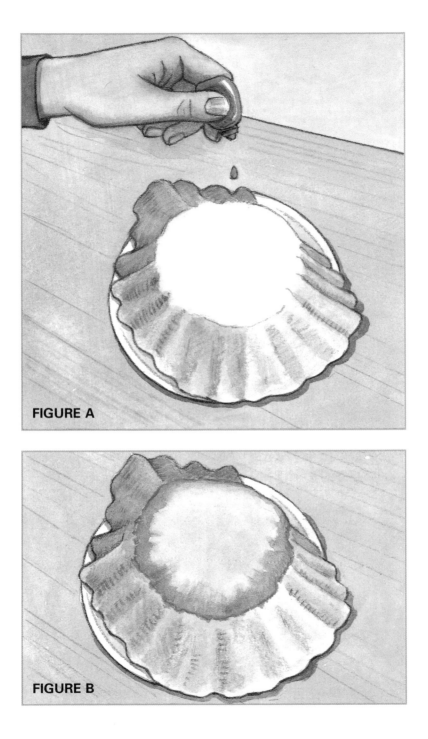

FIGURE A

FIGURE B

filter paper than the blue dye molecules. Therefore, the blue color spreads faster through the paper than the yellow. Between the yellow and blue there is a mixture of both types of molecules, and this area appears green.

The technique used in this experiment for separating colors is called *chromatography*. Chromatography is a way to separate substances in a mixture. A mixture of liquids or gases is passed through a solid that has a different attraction for the substances in the mixture. Those substances that have a strong attraction for the solid pass slowly through the solid. Those substances that have a weaker attraction for the solid pass through more rapidly.

Some types of chromatography include liquid chromatography, gas chromatography, and thin-layer chromatography. In liquid chromatography, a fluid is poured through a tube filled with a solid adsorbing material. As the liquid goes down the tube, it carries the mixture with it. In gas chromatography, a gas such as helium is flowed through a metal or glass column filled with solid. The flowing gas carries the mixture with it. In thin-layer chromatography, a mixture is placed on a flat sheet of an adsorbing solid. The adsorbing solid is placed in a liquid that spreads through the solid and carries the mixture with it.

In all three types of chromatography, as the chemicals or molecules in the mixture are carried through the solid, they are separated based on how strongly they are attracted to the solid. Which of the three types of chromatography described above did you do in your experiment?

Chromatography was invented in 1906 by a Russian botanist, Mikhail Semenovich Tswett. He named the technique chromatography, which means "writing in color." He used this technique to separate plant pigments (pigments are substances that give color). He washed the plant pigments through a column filled with powdered limestone and separated the pigments into bands of color.

We see some of these color pigments when leaves turn red, orange, or yellow in the fall. Chlorophyll, which gives leaves a green color, is no longer produced in certain trees in the fall, and so the color of other pigments present in the leaves can be seen. When these pigments are broken down, the leaves turn brown. Chromatography can be used to separate these colored pigments, which are present but cannot be seen in the leaves in the summer.

Chromatography is an important tool used by scientists to separate mixtures of chemicals and identify the types of chemicals in a mixture. Chromatography is used to determine the amounts and kinds of pollutant molecules in air and water, to determine the kinds of natural chemicals found in plants that may make useful medicines, and to identify the chemicals in unknown mixtures. Can you think of other ways that chromatography might be useful?

SCIENCE CONCEPTS

FURTHER READING

To explore further the properties of water and other liquids:

Ardley, Neil. *The Science Book of Water.* New York: Harcourt Brace Jovanovich, 1991.

Cooper, Christopher. *Matter.* New York: Dorling Kindersley, 1992.

Darling, David. *From Glasses to Gases: The Science of Matter.* New York: Dillon Press, 1992.

Gardner, Robert. *Experimenting with Water.* New York: Franklin Watts, 1993.

Mebane, Robert C., and Thomas R. Rybolt. *Adventures with Atoms and Molecules: Chemistry Experiments for Young People.* 4 vols. Hillside, N.J.: Enslow, 1985–1992.

———. *Environmental Experiments about Water.* Hillside, N.J.: Enslow, 1993.

Newton, David. *Consumer Chemical Projects for Young Scientists.* New York: Franklin Watts, 1991.

———. *Science-Technology-Society Projects for Young Scientists.* New York: Franklin Watts, 1991.

Peacock, Graham, and Cally Chambers. *The Super Science Book of Materials.* New York: Thomson Learning, 1993.

Sauvain, Philip. *Water.* New York: New Discovery Books, 1991.

VanCleave, Janice. *Janice VanCleave's Chemistry for Every Kid.* New York: Wiley, 1989.

INDEX

ABOUT THE AUTHORS

Rob Mebane teaches chemistry at the University of Tennessee at Chattanooga, where in 1990 he was a recipient of the Student Government Outstanding Teaching Award. He is the author of many articles in scientific journals and, with Tom Rybolt, has written fifteen nonfiction books for young people. Dr. Mebane lives in Chattanooga, where in his leisure time he enjoys white-water canoeing, backpacking, and cooking.

Tom Rybolt holds a doctorate in physical chemistry and is also on the faculty of the University of Tennessee at Chattanooga. He has written extensively for scientific journals, and in 1991 he was a recipient of the Student Government Outstanding Teaching Award. He lives in Chattanooga with his wife, Ann, and their four children, and enjoys reading, running, and raising children.